Hawaii...

For sheer beauty, it's unmatched.
In case your snapshots don't do this lovely island justice,
here's a picture book of memories to take home
so you can revisit the Big Island
with each turn of the page.

John Rooney

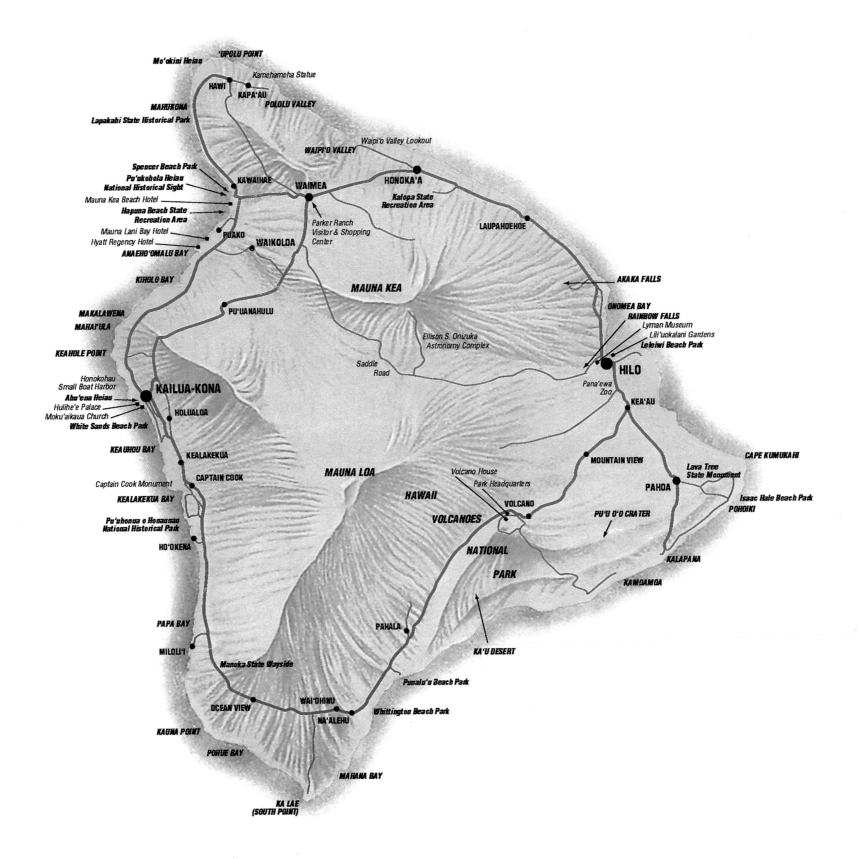

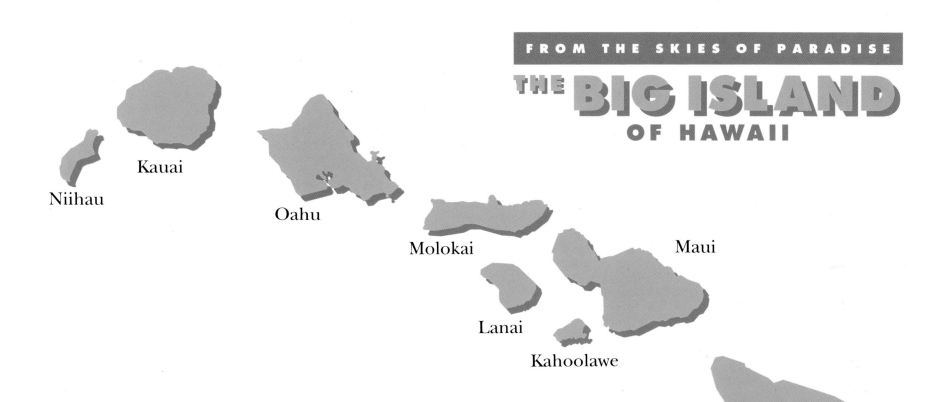

Niihau

Kauai

Oahu

Molokai

Lanai

Kahoolawe

Maui

FROM THE SKIES OF PARADISE

THE **BIG ISLAND**
OF HAWAII

Hawaii

FROM THE SKIES OF PARADISE

THE BIG ISLAND

OF HAWAII

Aerial Photography by Douglas Peebles

Text by Glen Grant

Mutual Publishing

PREVIOUS PAGE: *At the Mauna Kea Science Reserve observatories on the summit of Mauna Kea, and the lower-level Ellison S. Onizuka Astronomy Complex, astronomers from around the world have one of the best vantage points to study the heavens.*

FRONT COVER: *The spectacular lava fountains of Puʻu Oʻo cinder cone resemble a woman in a long red muʻu-muʻu shrouded in the white smoke of the eruption.* INSET: *The fingers of icy water cutting for tens of thousands of years through the Hamakua Coast hillside (now sugar covered) formed rugged coastlines such as Maulua Bay. Waipio Valley waterfall kissed by a rainbow.*

1 2 3 4 5 6 7 8 9
Second Edition June 1996

Printed in Taiwan
ISBN 0-935180-75-3
LCC 91-067614

Mutual Publishing
1127 11th Avenue, Mezz. B
Honolulu, Hawaii 96816
Ph: (808) 732-1709
Fax: (808) 734-4094
Email: mutual@lava.net
Url: http://www.pete.com/mutual

C O N T E N T S

From the skies, the landscape of the island of Hawai'i takes on a certain timelessness. Human efforts to mark the earth seem overwhelmed by nature. Magnificient beach resorts are reduced to miniature scale models laced together with a ribbon of tiny concrete highways along which ant-size vehicles inch. Villages where generations of Hawai'i's multicultural people have created their unique island lifestyle nearly disappear in the rugged terrain of ebony lava stone and verdant tropical foliage. In the midst of gently rolling pasture lands, a thousand-year-old stone edifice built by ancient Hawaiians appears almost as a *pohaku ki'i*, or petroglyph, a ghostly reminder of the civilization that once flourished in this land.

To see the earth from the summit as the gods do has been an ancient passion for land-locked humankind. In ancient Greek mythology, Daedalus and his son Icarus used wings made of feathers and wax to escape their prison on the island of Crete. Daedalus was successful; Icarus, despite his father's warning, flew too near the sun, melted his wings, and fell into the sea. For Polynesians who mastered the Pacific ocean currents and mapped the heavens, the desire to soar high above their island home was a similar source of imagination and mythic fancy.

If any Polynesian were to cut the bonds of gravity, it certainly would have been Maui, the trickster god who over the centuries continues to delight audiences of all ages with his often rascally exploits. It was Maui who, with *Manaiakalani*, the fishhook of heaven, accidentally lifted the Hawaiian islands from the bottom of the sea and then unsuccessfully tried to unite them into a single land mass. Who else but Maui could have lassoed the sun from the summit of Haleakala to slow its progress through the sky so that his mother Hina's tapa cloth could properly dry? To be the first Polynesian to see Hawai'i from the skies would be the herculean task, therefore, of Maui. Not that Maui's motive for flight was to pioneer aviation. He was simply attempting to rescue his wife Kumulama from Peapeamakawalu, the eight-eyed chief Peapea, who had the body form of a Hawaiian bat.

Today, our mastery of the skies with globe-circling spacecraft, transoceanic planes, and hovering helicopters may make the feats of Maui seem trivial. Every day the adventuresome leap from towering Hawaiian cliffs in hang gliders or parasail across tropical bays. The timeless vision is far more accessible than in the days of Maui, but it is no less awe inspiring. From the sky, the Hawaiian islands are stopped in eternity. Majestic volcanoes millions of years old, ringed by coral reefs set in azure seas, seem impervious to the busy human life moving insectlike across its face.

As we prepare to soar above the island of Hawai'i in **From The Skies of Paradise: The Big Island** to view its beauty and mystery from the perch of Maui's *mokumanu*, we are reminded of the old Hawaiian proverb, *Kukulu ka 'ike i ka 'opua*, "Knowledge is set up in the clouds."

*F*rom the Skies of Paradise: The Big Island of Hawai'i *is organized according to the* mokuaina, *or major land divisions, of old. The island of Hawai'i still accepts six major* mokuaina *divisions: Hilo, Hamakua, Kohala, Kona, Ka'u and Puna.*

Within these major land divisions were many ahupua'a, *smaller subdivisions, generally laid out* mauka *to* makai, *or from mountain to sea, according to tradition established over twenty generations ago. The* ahupua'a *boundaries were determined by identifying certain ecological variations within the area or native flora or fauna that inhabited a specific place. The chief given stewardship of the* ahupua'a *was responsible for controlling the distribution of its resources. The interdependency of those living within these areas formed the basis of the* 'ohana, *or family, where values of* kokua *or assistance,* lokahi *or harmony, and* aloha *or love, were taught.*

HILO & HAMAKUA

THE MAJESTIC WINDWARD COAST

Mauna Kea, snow-capped and brilliant in the clear morning sun, rises majestically above the Big Island's windward northeastern coast. In the verdant town of Hilo, yawning store-keepers are sweeping their front sidewalks. At the Suisan Fish Market prospective buyers inspect the night's catch of typically Hawaiian fish—*'ahi, aku, akule, mahimahi, 'opelu*—to be auctioned off in the next hour or so. Children of all sizes, shapes and ethnic backgrounds, many still rubbing the sleep out of their eyes, traipse off to school. Men in starched reverse *aloha* shirts and women in colorful *mu'u-mu'u*s head for the office. Kamehameha Avenue's distinctive storefronts on concrete and brick buildings—Main Street America with a Polynesian-Asian twist—come to life.

At the hotels along Banyan Drive, early-rising visitors sip Kona coffee and plot their day's excursion to Kilauea volcano. "A sunny morning in Hilo," they are told. "You're lucky." The 133 inches of rain that this district receives in a typical year has made Hilo famous. *Hilo i ka ua kinakinai, ka ua mao 'ole*, is an old Hawaiian saying. "Hilo of the constant rain, where it never clears up."

The criticism is unfair. After all, on an island where the sun usually is shining somewhere 365 days a year, the change of pace in Hilo is refreshing. The rains of Hilo are responsible for large, luxuriously green lawns and wildly growing shrubbery; thanks to the frequent veil of moisture, orchids and anthuriums of windward Hawai'i are world famous. Crisp, sunny, clear days are so special in Hilo that the color of everything takes on a new vibrancy.

When Mark Twain observed of Hawai'i that "other things change, it

PREVIOUS PAGES: *Guarded by snow-capped Mauna Kea looming in the distance, the Pacific town of Hilo grew from a quiet nineteenth century Hawaiian village into the island of Hawai'i's twentieth century urban center. Waiakea Pond in the left foreground flows into the spring-fed Wailoa River, the dominant waterway in a luxuriously landscaped 150-acre State recreation area.*

OPPOSITE: *With a 1990 population of some 48,000, Hilo has maintained its low-profile skyline with small town friendliness and a relaxed life style. A walk through downtown Hilo leads past wooden-front Japanese and Chinese stores and to simple stone structures transformed into modern cafes.*

Hilo, nahele paoa i ke ʻala—
Hilo, where the forest is imbued with fragrance
Hamakua i ke ala ʻulili—
Hamakua, land of tall cliffs

remains the same," he may have had Hilo in mind. Even with new shopping malls and business complexes, suburbs extending out toward Kilauea Volcano and up the Hamakua Coast, and a modern international airport, Hilo maintains a pace that's midway between the quiet of a Kaʻu village and the "relaxed hustle" of Kona. Some call it old-fashioned. Yet for those who enjoy the multicultural local scene, that fashion embodies the spirit of Hawaiʻi.

Northward along the Hawaiʻi Belt Highway, spanning the deep gulches for which Hamakua was famed in ancient chant and song, that "local" spirit lives on in the old sugar-plantation towns of Wainaku, Papaʻikou, Papaʻaloa, ʻOʻokala, Paʻauilo, Paʻauhau, and Honokaʻa. By noon the blades of sugar cane that stretch from the steep Hamakua cliffs up the slopes of Mauna Kea glisten in the sun. Cane-haul trucks turned red by the iron-rich soil, barrel along the highway stacked high with harvested cane destined for the mill. When sugar was king, the plantation towns teemed with immigrants from China, Japan, the Philippines, Puerto Rico, Okinawa, Korea, Portugal and the Pacific islands, whose tremendous labors made the Territory of Hawaiʻi wealthy. While building the economic foundations of the modern state, the immigrants and their offspring forged a chop suey way of life that today puts Japanese *sashimi* or raw fish, Filipino *lumpia* or spring rolls, Chinese *dim sum* or steamed dumplings, Hawaiian *poi,* Korean *kal bi* or barbecued beef ribs, and Portuguese *malasada*s or doughnuts—all washed down with American beer—on a normal menu.

The plantation lifestyles are changing along the Hamakua coast. Sugar is no longer Hawaiʻi's top economic industry. The current term popular for describing this shift in the island sugar industry is "down-sizing." With sugar's new reduced influence, so too have the plantation towns become "down-sized." The now retired, aging plantation workers find themselves watching their children and grandchildren move on to other islands,

Honolulu or even the mainland for job opportunities. The plantation stores where everything was once on a first name basis, are closing down. The Honpa Hongwanji congregations are falling off in size as the young people move on to other interests. What will become of Hamakua in the future as the older ways of life are replaced by the new subdivisions? Those kinds of questions are being asked more and more whenever the *kupuna* or elders gather at the senior centers or on the storefront benches in the cooling afternoon to "talk story."

Night falls in the remote Waipi'o Valley along the majestic windward coast. A full moon in an ebony-blue sky silhouettes a Pacific palm and illuminates a rolling evening surf. It's the classic South Seas scene—and it's real! Accessible by land only down a frightfully steep precipice, Waipi'o of ancient legend was the birthplace of Hawai'i's most sacred royalty. Once a populous village with hundreds of taro patches terraced back into the recesses of the valley, where the abundance of fish was legendary, Waipi'o today is hauntingly quiet. Only four-wheel-drive vehicles can scale the steep road, preserving the isolation. The few farmers who still grow their taro here in the ancient fashion invoke the protection of their *'aumakua*, or family spirits. This remote home is truly timeless, whether viewed from the land or the sky.

OPPOSITE: *Cascading 442 feet through a tropical rain forest of giant ginger, heliconia, ferns, orchids, and bamboo, Akaka Falls is one of Hawai'i's tallest waterfalls.*

LEFT: *Described in the last century as "a picturesque inlet, with residences along its shores," Reed's Bay, the largest natural bay along Hilo's shoreline, has become a popular boating harbor. On the Waiakea Peninsula (center), the famous Banyan Drive leads visitors to Hilo's largest hotels. The Naniloa Hotel stands on the point. On the western edge of Waiakea peninsula is the beautifully landscaped Japanese-style Lili'uokalani Gardens with a footbridge to Coconut Island.*

15

PREVIOUS PAGES: *Although frequently identified as a Hawaiian product, the native Australian macadamia nut actually was first introduced to Hawai'i at Honoka'a by W.H. Purvis in 1881. Thousands of acres have been converted to macadamia nut farms. Seven years must pass before a tree bears mature nuts which can be harvested only after they have fallen to the ground.*

RIGHT: *One of the features of Hilo is the frequent rainfall, averaging 133 inches a year, that helps to produce lush waterfalls such as these above Hilo. Water descending from the mountains irrigated the ancient Hawaiian taro cultivation systems. So essential was water to the well- being of a village that the word for wealth in Hawaiian is "waiwai," meaning abundant water.*

18

The time was just before midnight and the place was a desolate stretch of the Saddle Road that connects Hilo to the west side of Hawai'i across the island interior's lunar landscape. Taxi driver Pedro Monzano was returning to Hilo Airport after dropping a Parker Ranch employee at Humu'ula. Lava stones strewn across the road caused one of his tires to blow out.

After removing the lug nuts from his damaged tire, Pedro threw the wrench into the trunk of his car. As he lifted the spare tire onto the wheel, an extraordinary thing happened.

"I tighten the lug nuts when I hear a noise on the right side," he later told reporters. "I see the wrench. I stand up one time and look around. Nobody there."

Somehow, the wrench which had been in the car had moved out of the trunk to Pedro Monzano's side. Although terrified, he said out loud to no one in particular, "Thank you, very much." He then finished tightening his spare, jumped into his taxi, and sped to Hilo to spread the word about the ghostly doings on the Saddle Road.

Pedro Monzano wasn't alone in "seeing things" during February of 1969. A group of Department of Education teachers traveling on the Saddle Road earlier had seen eerie lights along the road. As they pulled over to examine the unusual phenomena, the strange fires vanished.

Akualele (literally, 'flying gods'), explained the Hawaiians of the Big Island. These fireballs that fly in the night are sometimes omens of approaching death. Local Japanese identified them as *hinotama*, or disembodied spirits.

The unearthly happenings on the Saddle Road did not begin with flying wrenches and fireballs. The Henry Macomber family, returning to Waiki'i from Hilo on the evening of January 31, 1969, saw two yellowish-red lights in the distance resembling an approaching car. The lights came closer, then suddenly vanished. Turning the pickup truck around to return to Hilo, the family was suddenly struck by an invisible force that rocked the vehicle violently. The terrified family then fled the scene of their supernatural encounter.

Henry Macomber later described for reporters how this powerful push seemed to have a mass. "It" struck the tarpaulin on the window, banged on the sides of the truck and rapped on the hood, he insisted.

Earthquakes? Swamp gas? Overactive imaginations? Despite the theorizing of Big Island scientists, no plausible explanation was given to Pedro Monzano, the teachers or the Macombers. What force could violently shake a pick-up truck or lift a wrench out of a trunk and throw it several feet? What are the *akualele* that Hawaiians for centuries have seen in the darkness of the night? What otherworldliness continues to haunt the Saddle Road?

Across the saddleback between the giant Mauna Kea and Mauna Loa volcanoes, a lonely two-lane highway links Hilo with Kona. With the gentle curves of Mauna Loa in the background, the Saddle Road cuts through volcanic landscapes, past the remote Pohakuloa military training area, and through regions that at night are inhabited by "akualele," mysterious fireballs, and vanishing hitchhikers.

RIGHT: *The largest of Hawai'i's native forest trees is the "koa" whose light-gray bark, crescent leaves and small white flowers can be seen here growing on the slopes of Mauna Kea. The fine red wood was used by ancient Hawaiians in the construction of canoes, bowls, and surfboards. In modern times it goes into furniture and "ukuleles." The long-term survival of many of Hawai'i's native trees is in jeopardy from over-cutting; reforestation of "koa," "iliahi" or sandalwood, "'ohia," and "kamani" is being attempted.*

OPPOSITE: *Rising from the Ke'amuku lava flow on the northern slopes of Mauna Loa, the Pu'u Kea ("White Hill") and Pu'u Ahi ("Hill of Fire") volcanic craters are visible in the Saddle area of Hawai'i. Although Mauna Loa has been relatively quiet in recent years, the volcano is still rated as active.*

22

PREVIOUS PAGES: *Snow-capped Mauna Kea (foreground) and Mauna Loa (looming in the distance) are Hawai'i's two greatest volcanic peaks. On the freezing summit of Mauna Kea the snow goddess Poli'ahu made her home while Pele the fire goddess reigned on Mauna Loa. Although Pele time and again hurled fiery rock and spewed lava toward Poli'ahu during their many battles, the ice maiden remained untouched in her cold and barren domain.*

RIGHT: *"Poli'ahu, ka wahine kapa hau anu o Mauna Kea," Poli'ahu, the woman who wears the snow mantle of Mauna Kea.*

26

Shrouded in low-hanging mist on the northeastern slopes of Mauna Kea, 'Umikoa, the Mauna Kea Ranch, is one of at least sixteen cattle "spreads" on the Big Island.

Tsunami, originally a Japanese word, is the now-accepted term for what people of all races on the Big Island most fear—the "tidal wave." Neither the volcano goddess Pele's destructive rage nor the earth-shaking tremors have caused as many deaths as have the unpredictable monstrous waves that in a single moment can obliterate a paradisiacal shoreline.

For the bustling little seashore community of Laupahoehoe, the word tsunami forever became etched in its collective memory on April 1, 1946. Tragedy came on a beautiful peaceful day. At seven o'clock in the morning many early risers were gathering on the beach to watch unusual sets of waves moving back and forth across Laupahoehoe Point. Marsue McGinnis, a teacher at the Laupahoehoe school situated near the rocky point, remembered later that the first waves were low and mild. They were followed by a succession of larger waves that kept receding further and further from shore. The fifth wave washed across the schoolyard, depositing fish all over the grass.

The children, just arriving for school, began gleefully gathering up the fine catch. Marsue and three other teachers went to their cottage behind the school to change for classes. What no one paid any attention to until it was too late was the next wave. It was building without end to an incredible height later estimated to be thirty feet. When at last the children and teachers realized their imminent danger, they fled inland.

Bolting out the back door of their cottage, the four teachers were hit by a massive wave that smashed the cottage and collapsed the roof. Marsue was pulled out to sea, riding the roof of the teacher's cottage like a raft. The next waves smashed it against the lava rocks and then pulled her out again as she clung to floating debris. Her three companions did not survive.

With all of Laupahoehoe's boats and canoes destroyed by the tsunami, rescue operations for the few survivors that were floating at sea were long delayed. It was evening before Marsue McGinnis was finally rescued through the daring efforts of Dr. Leabert Fernandez (who later married the young teacher).

Thirty-two people died that tragic morning in one of the worst tidal waves ever to strike the Hawaiian islands. Most of them were pupils and teachers of the Laupahoehoe school. The village never fully recovered from this disaster. Many of the town's people followed the new school in moving *mauka*, or mountainward, away from the peninsula. Today at the tip of quiet Laupahoehoe Point visitors find a small beach park and a memorial on the site of the ill-fated school. The names of the children and teachers who died on April 1, 1946 are remembered on this silent testimonial to the power of the sea and its influence on island history.

Laupahoehoe ("leaf of smooth lava") Peninsula was the result of a "holua," or sledding, contest that turned into a violent battle between the snow goddess Poli'ahu and the fire goddess Pele. Jealous of Poli'ahu's skill and the attention she was getting from the spectators, Pele sent a lava flow to destroy the home of her rival. With the help of snow and cold winds, Poli'ahu diverted the eruption down Laupahoehoe Gulch into the sea, forming the famous peninsula.

OPPOSITE: *The fingers of icy water cutting for tens of thousands of years through the Hamakua Coast hillside (now sugar covered) formed rugged coastlines such as Maulua ("difficult") Bay. Isabella Bird and other Victorian visitors traversing these gulches had to be lifted by rope up and down the sheer precipices.*

LEFT: *Traveling inland along the Hamakua Coast, passing through older sugar plantation villages interspersed with new housing and dodging the huge cane-haul trucks that frequently cross the highway, it is nearly impossible to see the natural drama taking place along the shoreline. Steep cascades and breath-taking vistas are best enjoyed from the air. "Hamakua i ka wakawaka," irregular and rough Hamakua, says the proverb praising the valleys and cliffs of this majestic land.*

31

ABOVE: *Pa'auhau community is at the end of a steep, potholed road that winds through acres of tall sugar cane near Hamakua. The well-shaded plantation homes surrounded by vegetable gardens, an occasional playing child and a few crowing cocks are remnants of the older, paternal plantation system. Workers from around the world* *eked out their lives here, saving for the sake of their children. The large plantation store and community hall are now quiet; the baseball field is empty; the number of simple wooden homes, once segregated by rank and race, has been greatly reduced. Pa'auhau today waits in a surreal quiet for a successor to once-great King Sugar.* OPPOSITE: *As the sugar industry is "down-scaled" and lands converted to visitor resorts or much-needed new housing, the aerial view of the Hamakua Coast will certainly be transformed. Rural plantation life is already fading as new roads connect little villages to expanding suburbs.*

The village of Honoka'a ("rolling (as stones) bay") is today best known as the "macadamia nut capital." Once a major sugar plantation town at the north end of the Hamakua Coast, Honoka'a still proudly maintains a "Filipino store," a "Japanese store," and a "Hawaiian store," echoes of its multicultural past. Except for the Dairy Queen "hang-out," Honoka'a still closes up on Sunday.

35

OPPOSITE: *Waipiʻo Valley, isolated by imposing cliffs and a rough, white-crested bay, is one of the last few vestiges of a Hawaiʻi tied to the "ʻaina," the land. The taro farmers of Waipiʻo pursue their livelihoods much as their forbears did when the valley was the home of the island's highest ranking Hawaiian chiefs including Liloa, ʻUmi, and the legendary Kamehameha.*

ABOVE: *To the north of Waipiʻo Valley, daring travelers enter remote, unpopulated Waimanu, Honokane Nui, Honokane Iki, Honokeʻa and Honopuʻe valleys. As late as the nineteenth century, Hawaiian villages could be found in each, but isolation and the discovery of*

alternative life styles finally left the area depopulated. Today only seabirds, along with a handful of hikers, hunters, archaeologists and refugees from civilization, find sanctuary on this stark coastline.

KOHALA

OF KINGS & PANIOLO

From the skies of paradise, most of the land of kings and *paniolo* seems like endless rolling volcanic hills and yellow lowland deserts, punctuated by splashes of fading green pastureland and ebony lava flows. On the ground, however, Kohala, the home of ancient Hawaiian chiefs and cowboys, is a startling set of cultural contrasts that convince first-time visitors that somehow, at the last intersection in Honoka'a, by turning left instead of right they have landed in the American West.

The senses can't be lying. Instead of the dramatic cliffs of Hamakua to the rear, the traveler now sees gently curving hills covered with grazing cattle and palamino horses more appropriate to Texas than to the Hawaiian Islands. Is that cactus growing there? Most remarkably, the air is suddenly ten degrees cooler, and the humidity has been replaced by a crispness that, when the sun sets, can cause teeth to chatter. Log cabins nestled among the ironwoods with columns of smoke twisting from their chimneys seem misplaced in a Pacific paradise.

Not only has the flora, fauna, and physical environment seemingly gone mad, but also the people. Stetson hats appear along with colorful snap-buttoned country-western shirts. Posters on the "old West" buildings announce next week's rodeo. As first-timers rub their eyes to make sure they aren't dreaming, a young woman of Hawaiian ancestry, decked out in cowboy fashion, rides up alongside them, dismounts, ties her chestnut pony to a hitching post, and strides proudly into the supermarket!

This is Hawai'i of the *paniolo*, or cowboy, who for a century and a half has ranched the uplands of Waimea. For if the *malihini*, or newcomer, observes closely, he will find that these men and women of the Kohala range

PREVIOUS PAGES: *The nineteenth century expansion of Hawai'i's cattle and sheep ranching (by the year 1900 to nearly 1,450,000 acres) transformed much of the Big Island into a vast pasture and firmly established the legend of the "paniolo," the Hawaiian cowboy.*

OPPOSITE: *"O Waipi'o me Waimanu, no 'oawa mahoe i ke alo o ka makani," Waipi'o and Waimanu, the twin valleys that face the wind. The stark ruggedness of upper Waipi'o Valley, carved by rain and wind, contrasts vividly with the easy grasslands of the mountains of Kohala in the distance.*

*K*ohala ʻaina ha'aheo,
Kohala, land of the proud.

with their distinctive feather-*lei* hatbands, pronounced pidgin English speech, and dignified bearing can only belong to the islands. Even their music, such as *"Puʻuhuluhulu,"* celebrating the roping of wild cattle, reveals that these *paniolo* are no mere replicas of the American cowboy. They are a hearty breed apart, fiercely proud of their heritage and their place in Hawaiʻi's history.

It is not difficult to find traces of the *paniolo* culture throughout Kohala, even as the land to the north transforms itself again into familiar tropical jungles and rocky coastlines. Ironwood windbreaks line the roads, interspersed with giant windmills and grazing cattle, sheep and goats (not to mention a llama ranch!). From Parker Ranch at Waimea to Kahua Ranch, Waiwailani Ranch and Ponoholo Ranch in the north, the upcountry road on Kohala mountain overlooks the distant Pacific in one of the most beautiful scenic rides on Hawaiʻi.

Dropping back down to the coast at Hawi, a new sense of island heritage becomes readily apparent. From the home of the *paniolo,* North Kohala transforms to the home of the great chiefs. Not only is this the land of Kamehameha, but of generations of leaders whose good-works and generosity became celebrated in the saying, *Lele o Kohala me he lupe la.*— Kohala soars as a kite. A visit to the Moʻokini *heiau* or temple at ʻUpolu Point is itself a sufficient reminder of the spiritual and cultural legacy of the Hawaiian people, their chiefs and priests. From that impressive rock edifice, which has stood since the twelfth century overlooking the channel between Hawaiʻi and Maui, emanates from every stone the *mana* or divine power that created the ancient civilization. As the Kohala winds sweep away the cloud cover, revealing distant Haleakala in all its splendor and a humpback whale passes the point, its broad tail slapping the sea with a resonate boom resembling a *pahu* or drum, the seeker of spirit finds an unearthly solace within the walled sacred temple.

From this ethereal sphere, it is easy in Kohala to transcend into the purely sensual realm where the royal luxury and status of old is given a new interpretation along the famous "Gold Coast." It is the last contrast awaiting the visitor in the *moku'aina* of Kohala—the fabulous resorts such as Laurance S. Rockefeller's exclusive Mauna Kea Beach Resort, the Mauna Lani Bay and Bungalows with its 18-hole championship Francis I'i Brown Golf Course, the fantasyland Hyatt Regency Waikoloa and the Royal Waikoloan. Each resort situated along beaches, coves, ancient fishponds and the old "King's Highway" through the lava-covered district, is a world unto itself, an elegant retreat from urban civilization. In the privacy of this separate universe, where the most pressing concerns are making sure the right amount of time is given to a golden tan or what par is the next hole, the spirit can indulge epicurean delights of cuisine, sunbathing, water sports, golfing, horseback riding and even swimming with dolphins. Even simple meditation finds no kinder home that the "Gold Coast" of Kohala.

In this land of kings and cowboys, all these contrasts become for the seasoned traveler a welcomed relief from a mundane world of sameness. From the *paniolo* branding pens of upcountry Waimea to the ancient village sites at Lapakahi, from the thirsty cactus of arid Kamuela to the jungle ferns of Pololu or from the humble plantation cottages of Kapa'au to the magnificent suites of the Kohala Coast, the diversity of Kohala is what enriches the people with a pride for their land, its heritage and its unfolding future.

OPPOSITE: *Waikiʻi Ranch in the southern district of Waimea extends into the drier lands of the Big Island that in recent years have been suffering a drought. Waikiʻi means "fetched water" in reference to a spring found in the area. The ancient hero Kamiki first brought water to this region when he traveled to Kawaihuakane, the "hidden water of Kane," and returned with a calabash of the cool "wai" which was transformed into a life-sustaining spring. New, ten acre homesites are now being developed on old Waikiʻi ranchlands as an upscale lifestyle of elegant estates, polo playing fields and country living evolves in the land of the Hawaiian cowboy.*

ABOVE: *Less than a quarter century ago, Waimea ("reddish water") was a ranching village of 2,000 people bothered more by stray cattle in the streets than by traffic. Today it is a bustling town of 10,000 with a new million-dollar Keck Observatory Center, an expanded Parker Ranch House tour, and traffic lights. Waimea's "paniolo" days are long gone.*

Hawai'i Preparatory Academy in Waimea is one of the island's top-rated private schools. Consisting of over 88 acres, the school's beautiful campus includes a swimming pool complex and the recently completed performing arts center. Originally begun in 1950 as an Episcopalian school for boys, Hawai'i Preparatory Academy has today an international co-ed student body.

The Hawai'i Belt Highway cuts
like a fault line through Parker
Ranch, the largest privately
owned cattle spread in the
United States. Founded by John
Palmer Parker I in 1847, the
225,000-acre Parker Ranch
has been passed through six
generations to its current owner,
Richard Smart. His 1862
"Hawaiian Victorian" home,
Puuopelu ("folding hills"), with
a world-class collection of
impressionist art, is open to
the public.

47

PREVIOUS PAGES: *Puʻu-Hue Ranch, named for 2,375-foot "hill of the gourd" in North Kohala, is one of nearly a score of ranches that make up the Big Island's contemporary cattle industry. In a century and a half of ranching, the traditional California-Mexican "wild west" cowboy has become a uniquely Hawaiian "paniolo" in "papale" hat woven of "lau hala" (pandanus) leaves, on a "noho lio" saddle with a "kaula ʻili" lariat in hand.*

RIGHT: *Looking like a row of children's pinwheels on a barren Kohala slope, the windmills of Kahua Ranch harness the famous winds that regularly blow through this northwestern corner of Hawaiʻi island to pump water to the new coastal resorts.*

The image of a Polynesian wearing chaps, spurs and a ten-gallon hat, riding the range, roping calves, and breaking broncos seems incongruous to a visitor caught off guard. Rodeos in the Paradise of the Pacific? Cowboys wearing a flower *lei*, driving cattle to palm-lined beaches and into a rolling surf to swim to waiting ships for transport to the stockyards? Stock Hollywood versions of the western cowboy run smack up against *na paniolo*, the rugged men and women who tend Hawai'i's ranchlands.

Hawai'i's cattle industry dates back to 1792 when Captain George Vancouver, the British navigator who followed Cook, presented horses and cattle to King Kamehameha I who, in turn, placed a *kapu*, or taboo, on the animals. So successful was the royal protection that in a short thirty years the cattle had formed tough, wild herds ranging throughout the island, destroying ground vegetation and endangering lives. Kamehameha III, himself capable of hunting down and roping wild cattle, lifted the *kapu* from the herds. Hawai'i's cattle industry became a reality when Spanish-speaking *vaqueros* were brought from Mexico to teach Hawaiians to ride the range on horses, to master the Mexican saddle, and to braid lariats. The California Spanish *vaquero* became the Hawaiian *paniolo*.

Then in the 1850s John Palmer Parker, a thirty-year resident of Hawai'i, acquired 1,640 acres of pasture land in the cool highlands of Waimea. After leasing the entire Waikoloa *ahupua'a* land subdivision, running from the mountain to the sea, the Parker Ranch became the largest in the islands. Today it is the largest privately owned ranch in the United States. The Parker dynasty transformed Waimea into rolling green pastures that seem incongruous alongside the lush jungles and barren lava of the Big Island. The Polynesian *paniolo* in time gave Waimea its reputation as a "cowboy town."

A rodeo in modern Waimea reflects Hawai'i's multiculturalism. Hawaiians, *haole* or Caucasian, Japanese, Chinese and Portuguese names are listed among the riders. Across the grass-covered lava hills of Waimea, on the slopes of Mauna Loa, Mauna Kea, Hualalai, and Kohala, a small but intensely proud breed of *paniolo*, whether riding horses, pick-up trucks, helicopters, or motorcycles, carry on a hundred-year-old tradition. They have adopted the trappings of the American "wild west," but always with a distinctive Hawaiian flair.

Seen from the skies above Kahua Ranch, a new "cell system" of cattle grazing leaves its distinct mark upon the land. Instead of in the traditional large rectangular paddocks, the cattle now feed in sixteen radiating pie-shape lots separated by electrified fences. Ideally, by the time the cattle have finally rotated from cell to cell through the system, the grass in the first cell will have grown back, ready to start a new cycle of grazing.

PREVIOUS PAGES: *Toward the summit of the Kohala Mountains, the Big Island's oldest extinct volcano, where deep-cutting streams bring water down from the wet uplands, the remnants of an ancient Hawaiian homestead remind us of the great civilization that once flourished in water-rich Kohala. How many Hawaiians lived in the islands before foreign diseases and cultural upheaval led to depopulation is a subject of heated debates. Estimates range from 200,000 to 1,000,000 "ka po'e kahiko," the people of old. In many areas, only these ghostly archaeological sites remain.*

RIGHT: *Multiple waterfalls cascade into remote upper Waimanu Valley in inaccessible northern Hamakua and Kohala districts.*

The waterfalls and deep, cold pools of the Kohala Mountains were important sources of irrigation water for ancient Hawaiian taro farmers and later the sugar plantations of the district. The Kohala Ditch, a twenty-two-mile tunnel and open waterway system that opened in 1906, carried upland water to coastal sugar plantations.

OPPOSITE: *From Pololu Valley the traveler through Kohala must abandon the automobile and continue in the time-honored tradition of Hawai'i—on foot. The steep, often muddy switchback trail used for centuries leads to a deserted cobblestone beach and high sand dunes lined by a grove of ironwoods.*

ABOVE: *From the air above the North Kohala coastline, Kauhola Point's lighthouse on the furthest tip of land is a white speck. Directly mauka, or mountainward, of Kauhola is the former Hala'ula sugar plantation and mill, closed in the 1970s. The only time Hala'ula sees traffic today is when the surf is up at Kauhola Point.*

In the twelfth century, legends say, Pa'ao, a priest, ordered the walls of Mo'okini Heiau (temple), erected possibly as early as 480 A.D., to be raised as high as thirty feet. In a single night, thousands of basalt stones were passed along a human chain stretching twelve miles from Pololu Valley to the temple site. Mo'okini Heiau, one of the more impressive religious sites on Hawai'i, today is under the protective stewardship of "kahu" Leimomi Mo'okini Lum. The small rectangular stone area above the temple complex is the traditional birthplace of King Kamehameha.

The sky was illuminated by a great star, the legends tell, on the "stormy night in November" when Kamehameha I was born at Kokoiki in the land called Kohala. His mother, Keku'iapoiwa, was traveling with the invading army of Alapa'i, a great Maui chief, when she went into labor. With rain, thunder and lightning filling the evening sky, she gave birth to a boy. Nae'ole, a Kohala chief, immediately snatched the child away and carried him to nearby Mo'okini Heiau. There the child, whom Nae'ole called Paiea ("hard-shelled crab"), was given blessings and sanctification.

Puzzled by the abduction of the chiefly infant, Alapa'i's men went through Kohala burning houses and searching for him along the way. When they learned that Nae'ole had taken Paiea, he was granted guardianship. Nae'ole's younger sister, Kekunuialeimoku, was appointed as his foster mother, according to Hawaiian custom.

Paiea spent his youth with Nae'ole, isolated in the remote Halawa hills of Kohala, learning the chiefly skills. His years there nurtured a certain aloofness that later gave him the name "the lonely one." When the young warrior finally emerged from his training to join his uncle Kalaniopu'u among the Kohala *ali'i*, or chiefs, his destiny was linked to the unfolding drama of Hawai'i's history. Kamehameha was at Kealakekua Bay to meet the British navigator named *Kapena Kuke* (Captain Cook), and to marvel at his technology of war. After defeating his rival cousins as the successor of Kalaniopu'u, Kamehameha built the great Pu'ukohola Heiau at Kawaihae and dedicated it to his war god, Kuka'ilimoku, whose image he always carried before his armies into battle. The invasions of Maui, Lana'i and Moloka'i islands followed in rapid succession. Then in 1795 the great battle for O'ahu secured his rule throughout Hawai'i except for the northwestern islands of Kaua'i and Ni'ihau. In 1810, the king of those last two islands agreed to come peacefully under Kamehameha's leadership, thus fulfilling ancient prophecies of a united island kingdom under a single great *mo'i*.

King Kamehameha's unification of the islands and his subsequent rule and diplomacy are so celebrated that today he seems larger than life. In the lonely hills and rugged shores of Kohala, however, Kamehameha comes alive again as a man who, in the struggles of his upbringing and rise to power, left his footsteps on the land he loved and called home. Following his death in 1819, his bones were concealed somewhere in Kohala. Fittingly "the lonely one's" final resting place is shrouded in mystery.

OPPOSITE: *Seventy-five years ago Mahukona was an important port to which the Hawaii Consolidated Railway daily carried tons of Kohala sugar for shipment to refineries. Closed during World War II and the victim of a deadly 1946 tsunami tidal wave, Mahukona's harbor facilities today are largely abandoned.*

ABOVE: *Few ancient sites are as accessible to the modern visitor as the Lapakahi State Historical Park. The original Hawaiian "ahupua'a" land division had a one-mile coastline and stretched "mauka" four miles to a height of 1,300 feet. Established in the thirteenth century, Lapakahi's center was the Koai'e fishing village* whose stone foundations for canoe sheds, fishing shrines, homes, sporting grounds, and eating houses are still visible from the air. The community was abandoned in the late 1800s after the streams were diverted for use by the sugar plantations. Only silent stones remain to tell the story.

RIGHT: *To fulfill his goal of conquering all the Hawaiian islands, Kamehameha the Great built Pu'ukohola ("hill of the whale") Heiau (temple) above Kawaihae Bay on the Big Island in 1790-91 and dedicated it to his war god Kuka'ilimoku. Recently restored by the U.S. National Park Service and rededicated as a religious site, its interior is accessible only to Hawaiian worshipers. In the foreground is the older Mailekini Heiau.*

OPPOSITE: *The 350-room Hapuna Beach Prince Hotel, the newest gem along the Kohala Coast, sits on a site featuring a series of underground springs, which would bubble to the surface during heavy rainfall, creating natural artesian fountains—thus the name "Hapuna," or "spring of life." This depiction has become the hotel's symbol, a series of curvilinear forms—gentle, friendly, and active.*

(Opposite photo courtesy of the Hapuna Beach Prince Hotel)

64

The Kohala Coast's first luxury hotel was Laurence Rockefeller's Mauna Kea Beach Resort, opened in 1965 on land leased from Parker Ranch. The smooth white crescent of Kauna'oa Beach, one of the Big Island's most beautiful, is home to the green sea turtle. Although no longer a Rockefeller property, the Mauna Kea Beach Resort, with a world-recognized collection of Asian and Pacific art, remains a standard of excellence.

66

The Orchid at Mauna Lani with more than 540 guest rooms, two championship golf courses, fine restaurants, and modern fitness amenities, give 21st-century meaning to Big Island hospitality.

RIGHT: *When the $70 million dollar, 350-room Mauna Lani Bay Hotel and Bungalows opened in 1983 on land and fishponds once owned by Francis I'i Brown, a much-respected part-Hawaiian businessman and sports figure, no visitor site in Hawai'i had ever cost so much for luxury—$200,000 for each room! Not only is it recognized for elegance, but the Mauna Lani has also been careful to preserve its rich historical heritage of Hawaiian sites, including ancient fishponds, petroglyph fields, and the Kings Highway trail that once ran the length of the Kohala coast.*

OPPOSITE: *The centerpiece of the Mauna Lani resorts is the 18-hole Francis I'i Brown championship golf course. The front nine holes are on rugged "'a'a" lava and the back nine on smoother "pahoehoe." The whole is as much an outdoor art form as it is a golf course.*

OPPOSITE: *Six miles inland from The Royal Waikoloan resort and the Hawai'i Belt Highway, the Waikoloa Village Golf Course offers 78 challenging traps of fine coral sand and two water holes in a course created by renowned designer Robert Trent Jones, Jr.*

ABOVE: *The Hilton Waikoloa is a fantasyland of lagoons with playful porpoises, enchanting waterways, water sports facilities, health spas, and secluded guest hideaways, all offering endless opportunities for recreation and celebration. It easily earns its title as "the most spectacular resort on earth."*

Situated along 'Anaeho'omalu
Bay, near the Ku'uali'i and
Kahapapa fishponds once
reserved for Hawaiian royalty,
the 523-luxury-guest-room
Royal Waikoloan offers access to
one of Hawai'i's better
white-sand beaches. The 150-
acre championship golf
course designed by Robert Trent
Jones, Jr. guarantees a vista
of mountains and sea from
every hole.

KONA
THE LAND OF LIVING HISTORY

Kona is a time tunnel for the adventurer through history. Where else is the full epic drama of the Hawaiian Islands more clearly told than along this hauntingly still leeward coastline famed for ever-present sun and azure seas? At the great Pu'uhonua-o-Honaunau religious complex, the unfolding of the spiritual system embraced by the ancient Hawaiians begins. How the *akua*, or gods, and *'aumakua*, or family spirits, created *lokahi*, or harmony, through the system of *kapu*, or sacred laws, is richly interpreted at Pu'uhonua-o-Honaunau, as is the compassion felt for the weak, the old or law breakers who could find sanctuary behind its walls. Misimpressions of what ancient Hawaiians believed concerning this world and the next are quickly dispelled through an understanding of the cosmology expressed at this "place of refuge."

Myths surrounding the first contact between modern Europeans and Hawaiians are seen in a new light at Ka'awaloa when the time traveler walks in the steps of Captain James Cook and Chief Kalani'opu'u. Somehow, Kealakekua Bay appears smaller than it should as the backdrop to such a momentous scene in history. Today sunbathers lounge on the fateful beach at Hikiau Heiau and others snorkel where H.M.S. *Discovery* and *Resolution* lay at anchor some two hundred years ago. The air that was filled with excitement then as thousands of Hawaiians welcomed the man they believed to be the god Lono seems incomprehensible today. Yet at shrub-covered, deserted Ka'awaloa, accessible only by water, the true events of 1779 seem strangely real. Time stands still where Captain Cook urged Kalani'opu'u to step to the shore where a detachment of British marines hoped to hold the great chief until a boat stolen earlier that day was returned. Turmoil erupted as distant

PREVIOUS PAGES: *Kailua Bay (left) and Oneo Bay at the foot of Hualalai Volcano were the setting for historic Kailua village. The great King Kamehameha spent his last days here. Today Kailua-Kona is the Big Island's fastest growing community and a major visitor destination, with new suburbs, resorts and industries.*

OPPOSITE: *The truly exclusive Kona Village Resort on secluded Ka'upulehu Bay just north of Kailua-Kona town is celebrated for its Polynesian hospitality. Far from telephones, television or radio, the retreat is for those seeking "hale pili" (grass house) accommodations. "Beachcomber bungalows" promise guests the tranquility of Hawai'i a hundred years ago.*

Kona, kai ʻopua i ka laʻi.
Kona, where the
horizon clouds rest
in the calm.

cannon fire was heard. Were the foreigners killing natives? Would they try to kill Kalaniʻopuʻu next? Blows ensue, clubs are wielded, then musket fire is heard and in one swift tragic moment the circumnavigator falls, mortally wounded. The immediacy of the past is everywhere chilling, especially in Kona where blame and guilt have been heaped.

Kamehameha's spirit also is everywhere alive in Kona. The sites of his great battles dot the maps; the legends of his heroism and compassion are told by the *kupuna,* or elders. At the King Kamehameha Hotel in Kailua-Kona, the temple of Ahuʻena within which the great king died in 1819 has been reconstructed. Closed to visitors, its grass houses and oracle tower, ringed with large wooden *kiʻi,* or images of dieties, stand as a silent reminder that Kona has a rich Hawaiian legacy.

That legacy is evident also at the first Protestant place of worship erected in the Hawaiian Islands. Kailua-Kona's Mokuaikaua Church was established in 1820 by the first company of Congregational missionaries sent by the American Board of Commissioners for Foreign Missions. From here they sent out emissaries to plant "the true vine of God." Directly across the road is the Big Island's only nineteenth century royal palace, Hulihee Palace, built in 1838 by Governor John Adams Kuakini.

The Kona story also involves coffee farmers and ranching.

What Mark Twain called "one of the most delicious coffees in the world," first cultivated on the slopes of Hualalai Volcano, provided independent income for enterprising Chinese and Japanese immigrants fleeing the poor wages of the sugar plantations. The old wooden Buddhist temples, the crowded graveyards on the *mauka* roads of Hualalai, and the shop names in the coffee villages of Holualoa, Honalo, Captain Cook and Napoʻopoʻo tell of generations of Asian immigrants who have contributed to the Kona legend.

At the Greenwell Store in Kainaliu you can touch the *paniolo* past in

the form of such artifacts as saddles, ranch equipment, coffee grinders and old milk bottles—material evidence of the multicultural richness of Kona's people, their dependency upon the land for sustenance, and their struggles to understand one another with the old Hawaiian spirit of *aloha*.

To understand that special spirit, descend to the fishing village of Ho'okena along a narrow, sometimes gravel road that cuts off from the main Kona highway. At the end of the road, a clump of open-aired, old-style wooden houses are interspersed among the palms and shade trees. Located right along the beach is a three-story, grass-thatched complex with connected apartments that comprise the Hale Kai bed-and-breakfast, an intriguing getaway that almost has the appearance of something out of Paul Theroux's *Mosquito Coast*. Next to the ruins of the old boat landing at Ho'okena, two little Hawaiian girls tend their parents cold-soda shack, although they are not yet certain how to make correct change so they must frequently call their older brother. A group of three Ho'okena residents — part-Hawaiian, Filipino and Japanese—enjoying a cool beer in the heat of the day, sit under the shade of a beach pavillion, "talking story" about everything under the sun. Along the beach, a few *haole* tourists who have discovered Ho'okena spread out their lounge chairs on the beautiful but small patch of white sand. A noisy group of Hawaiian children are frolicking in the surf that gently laps up against this black lava coastline that has seen a thousand years of human history. A family outfits their homemade canoe to ready it for *'opelu* fishing—the kids roll up the nets and mother cleans out the cooler while the patriarch and his friends are carrying the canoe down to the water. And then two thoughts suddenly strike the observer of this tranquil scene—Hawai'i without her people is scenery without soul. Kona without knowing its history, is a land without meaning.

Along the North Kona coast
many deserted beaches await the
adventuresome. Inaccessible
except on foot or in a canoe,
these secret bays are reminders
that this wild, rugged part of
West Hawai'i has not been
totally tamed.

OPPOSITE: *On 20,000-acre Puʻuwaʻawaʻa Ranch at the base of Puʻuwaʻawaʻa ("furrowed hill") about 2,500 head of cattle are tended by only five "paniolo" cowboys. Started a century ago by colorful one-handed, cowboy-politican Eben Low, the spread is famous for the endurance of the men who work its ranges.*

ABOVE: *The lonely summit crater of 8,271-foot Hualalai Volcano appears to be long extinct. Actually, the U.S. Geological Survey lists Hualalai as the fourth most dangerous volcano in the United States. Seismic activity indicates that the mountain, which last erupted in 1801, has the potential for a Mount St.Helen-type eruption.*

Kahoupokane was the goddess of Hualalai mountain during its long dormancy. Poliʻahu reigned as the snow goddess of Mauna Kea, visible in the distance (left), while Pele the fire goddess had her throne on Mauna Loa (to the right). Powerful and vindictive Pele, however, set Hualalai afire in 1801. A torrent of lava sped to the sea in North Kona, consuming everything in its path with astonishing power.

Kamehameha, the great chief of Kohala, first defeated his cousin Kiwalaʻo at Mokuʻohai near Kealakekua Bay in South Kona, claiming for himself the rich north and western sides of the island of Hawaiʻi. Then another cousin, Keoua, marched his army against him, camping en route near Kilauea Volcano. The action angered Pele, the volcano goddess, who looked with favor on Kamehameha. She showed her wrath by causing a violent eruption that engulfed Keoua's army in deadly gases and fiery lava. To this day, hikers see the "footsteps" of Keoua's troops who, with feet bound in *ti* leaves, fled across the lava.

Although she had helped to defeat Keoua's army, Pele became jealous of young Kamehameha who had now gained political control of the entire island. As she watched the king enjoy his fishponds at Kiholo and Kaʻupulehu and bathing pools along the Kona coast, she became determined to destroy the things from which he gained so much pleasure. Thus in 1801 she aroused sleeping Hualalai Volcano, which sent a torrent of lava to threaten Kamehameha's favorite fishponds.

The native Hawaiians fled from the fiery river. Priests, seers and orators failed to appease the goddess. What had so aroused her wrath? One of Pele's priestesses revealed that the goddess felt neglected. Hadn't she blessed Kamehameha's efforts in battle by defeating Keoua? Yet what special honor had he paid her? Kona was doomed unless the great Kamehameha humbled himself to Pele.

Realizing that, unless he made a sacrifice, the lava of Hualalai would overrun all that he loved, Kamehameha made a pilgrimage to the flow's furthest point of advance. Cutting a lock of his sacred hair, the great king offered it as a symbol of his own *mana*, or divine power. The flow stopped almost immediately. Many present said that, as the lava cooled to stone at Kamehameha's feet, Pele, herself as a beautiful woman, led a procession of goddesses in human form in performing a *hula* before the conqueror of the islands. King Kamehameha had learned the value of humility.

RIGHT: *An outrigger canoe paddles past the Royal Kona Resort in the popular waters off Kailua-Kona. The landmark 445+ room terraced resort boasts of five golf courses, a private snorkeling lagoon, and spectacular views of coastline and sea.*

OPPOSITE: *One of several new developments at Keahou Bay south of Kailua-Kona, the popular Kona Surf Resort and Country Club on a private 14-acre peninsula offers salt and freshwater swimming pools, a 27-hole golf course, and 537 rooms and suites that overlook historic Keauhou community.*

86

ABOVE: *The coffee orchards of upcountry or mauka Kona once dominated not only the scenery but the lifestyles of West Hawai'i residents. Kona "nightingales" or donkeys loaded down with bales of aromatic coffee beans moved in caravans along the roads while independent Japanese and Chinese farmers enlisted their whole family to* pick the beans during the *harvest. Even the Kona schools changed the students' summer vacations to fall recess so as to accommodate the coffee harvests. It was in this region of coffee fields and upcountry villages that Ellison S. Onizuka grew up to one day become Hawai'i's own astronaut.*

OPPOSITE: *Cobblestone Ka'ohe Beach, known to South Kona "kama'aina," or old timers, as Pebble Beach, fronts the ocean at a new subdivision in a remote stretch of coastline between Ho'okena and Miloli'i, south of Kailua-Kona.*

The two floating islands whose great trees were draped with white *tapa* and that carried men with strange angular heads, flashing eyes and breaths of fire, anchored in Kealakekua Bay at a most propitious time. The annual *makahiki* celebrations, to rejoice in the bounty of the harvest and to honor the god Lonoikamakahiki, had just begun. Once a great chief who had slain his spouse in a jealous rage and then had lost his mind in grief, Lonoikamakahiki had journeyed to the spirit world, vowing to return when he had found her. The people of Hawai'i used the weeks-long *makahiki* festival to pay homage to Lono through feasting, dancing, songs, games, and processions. Priests carried the symbol of Lono, long strips of white *tapa* hanging from tall crosses. In fact, they exactly resembled the banners rising above the floating islands. Was this the long-awaited Lono?

Aboard the islands was a great chief. Fair-skinned and regal in bearing, was this not Lonoikamakahiki? Certainly his *mana*, his divine power, was very great. He carried sticks which spewed steam; when pointed at a man, the sticks could kill him. Red-mouthed tree trunks gushed smoke and a stone that leveled a house. Everywhere were rocks that held a sharp edge. Called *pahoa*, iron made an excellent knife or spearpoint. The wrinkled skin and angular heads of these foreigners turned out to be sturdy clothes and unique three-corner hats. Their shiny eyes were worn to improve their vision and the fiery breath was from smoking tobacco or pipes.

The great chief of the floating islands was received at Kealakekua as Lono. He was draped in beautifully crafted feather capes and sanctified at the great temple. Everywhere he went, people bowed and called out, *Ke Akua Lono, Ke Akua Lono*, "The god Lono, the god Lono."

Thus was the famed British circumnavigator Captain James Cook received on the island of Hawai'i in January 1779. A year earlier, when his ships first sighted the previously uncharted Hawaiian islands, he had touched at Waimea, on Kaua'i, but his real introduction to the people was to be at Kealakekua where he and the crews of H.M.S. *Resolution* and *Discovery* would spend a happy, peaceful month. Hawai'i had experienced its first contact with the West and both parties seemed pleased at the prospect of trade and friendship.

It is ironic that such a peaceful first contact should have ended on February 14, 1779 in an outburst of violence that left Hawaiians, several British seamen, and Captain Cook himself dead along the shore at Ka'awaloa. A solitary white obelisk that commemorates Captain James Cook, R.N. stands today beside the bay at Kealakekua as a symbol of a peace marred by misunderstanding, and as a harbinger of an advancing civilization that was to overwhelm the people of old.

Along the haunted shores of Ka'awaloa, on Kealakekua Bay, a small pier and a white monument erected in 1874 to the memory of Captain James Cook are clearly visible. Near here on February 14, 1779 the British circumnavigator was killed when a misunderstanding turned tragically violent.

OPPOSITE: *Pu'uhonua-o-Honaunau, an ancient "place of refuge," was one of the most sacred areas on the Island of Hawai'i. Within its walls violators of the "kapu" laws sought sanctuary and purification, and women, children, the elderly and the weak found protection during war. Preserved and interpreted today by the* U.S. National Park Service, *reconstructed historic sites such as the large "pili"-grass Hale-o-Keawe bone mausoleum visible along the bay can be examined.*

ABOVE: *From the beach at Ho'okena, once a major South Kona port, Hawaiian families still set out in canoes to net "'opelu," or mackerel scad, and "akule," or big-eyed scad. Parents and children working together to bring in their weekly fish supply keep alive the old Hawaiian saying, "Ua ola no o kai ia kai," Shore dwellers find subsistence in the sea.*

A grass-roofed "hale pili" house, facing Ho'okena's lava-covered beach, is actually an island hideaway for adventure photographers David Blehert and Debbie Koehn called Hale Kai ("House of the Sea"). As is true in many remote parts of the Big Island, traditional ways often must blend with unrelenting progress.

95

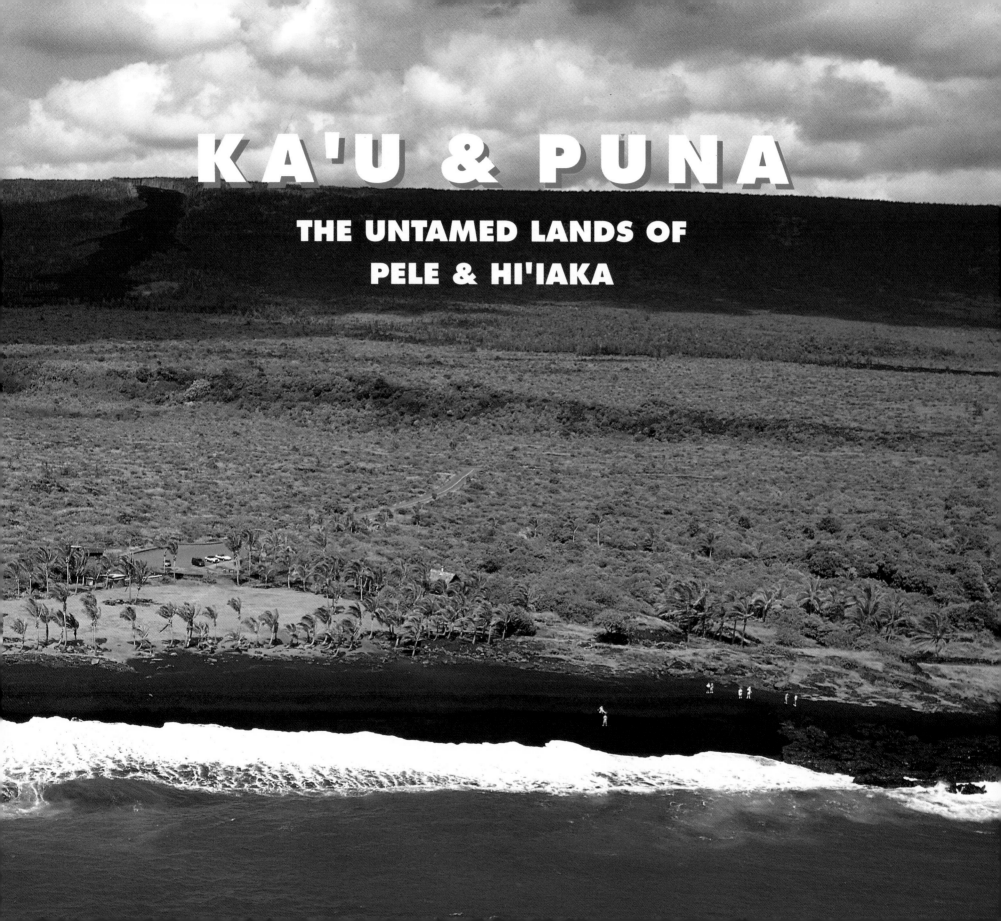

KA'U & PUNA

THE UNTAMED LANDS OF
PELE & HI'IAKA

Ka wahine ʻai honua, the earth-eating woman, came to Hawaiʻi from Kahiki, the land of her origin, following the male deities Kane, Kanaloa, Ku and Lono. This red-eyed woman, Pele, brought her brothers and sisters, including Kamohoaliʻi, the shark god. They landed first on Kauaʻi, then moved to Kaʻena Point on Oʻahu. Pele, always seeking the fires of the earth, struck Oʻahu with her digging stick at several places but found no volcanic activity. She journeyed on. In Puna, on the island of Hawaiʻi, the goddess struck the earth at Halemaʻumaʻu within Kilauea Crater. A lake of fiery lava bubbled up. Greatly pleased, the woman said to eat stone had found her home of fire.

Living with Pele at Kilauea were her twelve sisters all of whose names began with "Hiʻiaka." The youngest and most loving was Hiʻiakaikapoliopele ("Hiʻiaka in the bosom of Pele"). Legends speak of Pele's having carried her as a feather or an egg nestled in her bosom. It was always Hiʻiaka who volunteered first to do Pele's bidding.

One time Pele fell asleep while bathing in Puna and traveled in her dream to the island of Kauaʻi. There she saw and fell in love with Lohiʻau, a handsome young chief. When she awoke on the beach in Puna, Pele asked if one of her sisters would travel to Kauaʻi to fetch this young mortal. It was Hiʻiaka, of course, who assented to the dangerous journey.

"Return within forty days with Lohiʻau untouched," Pele admonished her sister, "or I will cover your beautiful groves and destroy your good friend, the dancer Hopoe of Keaʻau."

On Kauaʻi, Hiʻiaka learned that Lohiʻau had committed suicide over the sudden disappearance of the mysterious woman with whom he had

PREVIOUS PAGES: *Kamoamoa fishing village in the Puna district east of Hilo was swept in 1868 by a devastating tsunami tidal wave, leaving only the ruins that are still visible near the low black lava cliffs.*

OPPOSITE: *Ka Laʻe or remote South Point in Hawaiian legend is said to be where the first human beings settled in the Hawaiian islands. The extensive archaeological remains in the area makes Ka Laʻe one of the most important areas on the island to interpret the ancient civilization of Hawaiʻi.*

Hilinaʻi Puna kalele ia
Kaʻu, hilinaʻi Kaʻu kalele ia Puna.

Puna trusts and leans on Kaʻu,
Kaʻu trusts and leans
on Puna.

fallen in love. Hiʻiaka the healer restored him to life and persuaded him to make the perilous trip back to Puna. The days had passed too quickly, however. In Puna, jealous Pele had poured destructive lava over Hiʻiaka's forests and had turned Hopoe into a balancing rock that seemed to dance along the shoreline at Keʻeau.

When Hiʻiaka and Lohiʻau reached the Big Island and saw the devastation, the younger sister was filled with fury.

"I manai kau, i pua hoʻi kaʻu, kui ʻia ka makemake a lawa pono," Hiʻiaka said to the handsome chief as they stood at the edge of Kilauea Crater. "Yours the *lei*-making needle, mine the flowers; so let us do as we wish." They embraced to make the complete *lei*. Pele exploded. Running for his life, Lohiʻau was overtaken by molten lava and turned to stone. Invulnerable to lava, Hiʻiaka was unscathed. The happy ending to the tale is that Hiʻiaka later was reconciled with Pele, and the ghost of Lohiʻau was resurrected for the pleasure of Hiʻiaka.

From this and other episodes, humans who lived in Puna and Kaʻu learned of Pele's stormy temperament and that their proximity to the volcano goddess was a source of danger. Before the arrival of Pele, it was said, Puna was *ke one lauʻena a Kane*, the rich, fertile land of Kane. Her selection of Puna as a home changed the land to lava, cinders, and rock. The awe of Pele extended to never eating the native *ʻohelo* berries at Kilauea without first offering some to the goddess, lest the land be shrouded in rain and fog.

"Wrongdoing is feared in the upland of Puna," said the people of old. It also aroused the anger of Pele!

What comforts those who live in fear of Pele's temper is that her youngest sister Hiʻiaka brings the destroyed earth back to life with her healing powers. The gentle sister nurtures the propagation of flowers, plants and the native ferns in her medicinal arts. *"Ola no i ka pua o ka ʻilima,"*

explains the Hawaiian proverb, "there is healing in the *'ilima* blossoms." The delicate, orange *'ilima* was the flower frequently used by Hi'iaka who gave the juice of the blossom as a mild laxative to infants as their first medicine. So has the goddess of healing covered Puna with the large endemic tree fern *hapu'u* and the smaller, simple fronds of the *'ama'u*. In her green canopied rainforests, Hi'iaka has spread the native *'ohia* to give forth fresh air for a world wearied by pollution.

Pele and Hi'iaka, working together, have made Puna and Ka'u, among the newest lands on earth, the most untamed. Varying from deserts created by volcanic "acid rain" and blackened, barren lava fields in Ka'u to the wild rainforests of Puna filled with many of the few remaining endangered native Hawaiian birds and marvelous insects, the two sisters have created some of the most spectacular natural beauty ever enjoyed or feared by mortals. In this mythological land of the gods, modern *kama'aina*, residents must continually revere the power of Pele and welcome the supplicant beneficence of Hi'iaka. And in turn, the gods reciprocate with their special obligation to human life. For as Hi'iaka once told her older sister:

"E malama i ka iki kanaka, i ka nu'a kanaka. O kakou no keia ho'akua."

"Take care of the insignificant and the great people.

That is the duty of us gods."

The green olivine sand beach at Ka La'e ("South Point"), the southernmost spot in the United States, is renowned. Surf beating on the base of Pu'u-o-Mahana has washed fine grains of the light-green volcanic mineral olivine from the cinder cone to collect in pockets along the shore. The mineral-rich Big Island has black, brown, gray, white, and green-sand beaches, some with sprinklings of red.

Mysteries surrounding stones abound on the Big Island. The bad luck reputedly suffered by those who take home home lava fragments from Kilauea volcano, for example, is so pervasive that overseas visitors frequently mail back boxes of the black rocks taken as souvenirs. Letters accompanying the rocks often tell of ill fortune or even supernatural occurrences that convinced the rock collector that these Hawaiian stones belong back in the land of Pele.

While Pele's lava pieces may resist wandering off, other *pohaku*, or stones, are said to possess different marvelous properties. *Kupua*, or spirits, inhabit certain rocks, and some even can prevent humans from lifting them. Sacred birth stones supposedly absorb a mother's pain at childbirth while other rocks are respected for their ability to heal, assure growth, or excite fertility. At Waikupuna in Ka'u on the Big Island, *pohaku wa'uwa'uili*, "stones that claw the skin," are said to be extremely effective as a love potion.

Of the many sacred stones found in Hawai'i, perhaps none are as puzzling as the *pohaku hanau*, or the stones that give birth, found especially near the Big Island's green sand beach at South Point. The earliest recorded observation of such stones came from the London missionary William Ellis who in 1823 circumnavigated the island of Hawai'i and noted that at Ninole people showed him rocks "which were reported to possess very singular properties; amongst others, that of propagating their species." The missionary, of course, dismissed the information, adding that "it required all the argument and ridicule that we could employ, to make them believe it could not possibly be so." Yet many persist in their faith that certain sacred stones at Ninole would indeed produce children.

Kupuna, or elders, from the region today describe these marvelous stones as smooth, sausage-shaped and small enough to be held in the palm of the hand. Although the stones are heavy and solid, one small spot feels pliable when pushed with the thumb. This is explained as the rock's *piko*, or belly-button. When the stone is left undisturbed for several days and certain prayers are offered, a small pebble is often found at the *piko*.

To western minds, tales that stones may possess spirits or heal the sick or give birth to children defy scientific belief. *He ola ka pohaku*, "There is life in the stone," is an old Hawaiian saying.

103

ABOVE: *The fishing village of Ka'iliki'i was abandoned in 1868 when Mauna Loa sent a devastating lava flow into the area, destroying the fringes of the village. Two stone foundations, a high-walled canoe shed in the foreground and, immediately above, what is believed to be a community house, remain.*

OPPOSITE: *Pu'u O'o cinder cone formed when an eruption began January 3, 1983 on the southeastern flank of Kilauea Volcano. The flow has continued unabated to this day, spewing out nearly 650,000 cubic yards of magma every 24 hours. U.S. government scientists with video cameras keep close tabs on the cinder cone's activity, providing important information on what is certainly one of the most active volcanoes in the world.*

RIGHT: *This view into a lava tube through a "skylight" window offers a glimpse of the river of 2,000-degree magma that poured over Kapaʻahu and Kalapana communities and obliterated more than 100 homes, as well as roads, shops, churches and beach parks.*

OPPOSITE: *The spectacular lava fountains of Puʻu Oʻo cinder cone resemble a woman in a long red muʻu-muʻu shrouded in the white smoke of the eruption. In its first three and a half years, Puʻu Oʻo erupted 47 times, creating a cone 830 feet high with a pit 1,000 feet across. The action later moved downslope, but continues to the present day.*

106

OPPOSITE: *When Pele, the fire goddess, bathes in the sea, the ocean boils. Small drops of still molten lava are hurled into the air to cool into tiny grains of volcanic glass that accumulate on Hawai'i's famed black-sand beaches.*

ABOVE: *Lava consuming the Puna coastline is dramatic evidence of the goddess Pele's unceasing creation of new land. "Pau Puna ua ko'ele ka papa," Puna is ravaged; the foundation crackles.*

The walk from where the recent lava flows have covered the Chain of Craters Road to Waha'ula Heiau, a twelfth century Hawaiian temple, today requires forty-five minutes over *'a'a* and *pahoehoe* lava. A few years ago visitors to this most sacred religious site could have driven into the convenient parking lot of the U.S. National Park Service interpretive complex. They would have enjoyed a modern facility which explained the meaning of Waha'ula ("red-mouth") temple, its important use as a *luakini* or human sacrificial altar, and the dedication by Kamehameha I of the site to his war god, Kuka'ilimoku.

As the hiker approaches Waha'ula, what appears as the skeleton of a large beached whale rises in the distance. Four tall palm trees without leaves stand like unstrung telephone poles. The "beached whale skeleton" turns out to be the metal frames of the Park Service visitor center destroyed by the intense heat of the approaching lava. The truncated palms grow out of a patch of earth on the seaside of the ancient stone wall of the heiau that remained untouched by the lava. Examination of the space between the walls of the historical structure and the now-solid lava reveals that the magma came within inches of Waha'ula before halting. In an ocean of black rock, unrelenting in its destruction throughout Kalapana, a miraculous oasis of spiritual heritage stands unmarred.

Many are the contemporary legends of how the goddess Pele spared this house or that family from her destructive force of fire. At Kumukahi Point during the Kapoho eruptions in 1960 a light tower was saved with only inches to spare from the advancing lava. Apparently the keeper had befriended an old Hawaiian woman the night before Kapoho erupted. The sighting of a beautiful young women in a white dress, accompanied by a white dog, who suddenly disappears, is a sign to some that an eruption soon will follow.

Recently, a rescue helicopter pilot saw an old Hawaiian woman sitting on the back *lanai* of a Kalapana house about to be destroyed by lava. When he landed he informed the waiting family of the old woman he had seen from the air. They were puzzled. There was no woman, they informed him. And, indeed, no old woman was ever found although her only retreat would have been either past the pilot or through the lava.

Did Pele spare Waha'ula Heiau so that future generations would know the things of the past? Did she stop the flow because, as a woman during her menstrual cycle, she was not allowed into the temple under the old *kapu* system? Or was it merely a coincidence that the lava circled the temple and left it untouched? Standing in the midst of this "coincidence" one wonders at the marvelous power of Pele and her uncanny sense of will.

Waha'ula Heiau (temple) appears as a small stone oasis in a sea of lava in this eerie glimpse of the extraordinary power of Pele the volcano goddess to destroy, yet spare certain structures in her relentless advance.

111

ABOVE: *Introduced into the Hawaiian islands in the late eighteenth century, goats soon turned wild and created havoc for native flora. In the 1920s the Hawaiian Volcanoes National Park organized large-scale goat drives in the Kalapana and Ka'u districts, attempting to eradicate the destructive animals. Nevertheless, despite continuing effort some wild goats still eke out an existence on remote lava flows.*

OPPOSITE: *Residents of Kalapana and Royal Gardens Subdivision watched helplessly as lava consumed historic landmarks, the popular Queen's Bath swimming hole, and more than a hundred homes. The famed Painted Church of Kalapana escaped when the community united to lift it out of the path of the advancing lava.*

OPPOSITE: *Halape Beach is in a beautiful white sand cove separated by a powerful longshore current from the Ke'a'oi Island State Seabird Sanctuary. This seemingly peaceful site, however, was hit in 1975 by a deadly tsunami tidal wave that killed two campers.*

LEFT: *Volcanic eruptions in 1955 and 1960 destroyed the old village of Kapoho despite desperate efforts to divert the lava flow. Kapoho Bay, however, was spared and has become a popular site for beachfront homes. The rough lava-covered coast provides residents with private fishponds and tidal pools that regularly refill with fish, shellfish, crabs, and sea cucumbers.*

115

A controversial geothermal development rises prominently amidst the Puna rain forest. Plans to develop geothermal energy are heralded by some as an important alternative source of energy and condemned by others as a potential environmental disaster as well as an affront to the goddess Pele.

117

OPPOSITE: *Where Pele's fire has created barren rock on the Puna coastline, her sister goddess Hi'iaka creates verdant landscapes.* "Puna, kai nehe i ka ulu hala," *Puna, where the sea murmurs to the pandanus grove.*

ABOVE: *Arching over the Green Lake of Kapoho, an* "anuenue," *or rainbow, signals that the gods are watching the chiefs.* "Kau ka 'onohi ali'i i luna," *The royal eyes rest above.*

FOLLOWING PAGE: *Black sand beaches along the lush Puna coast are among the newest untamed lands of the earth.* "He lani i luna, he honua i lalo," *Heaven above, earth beneath.*

119

The Big Island is the most interesting of the Hawaiian Islands from the air. In a helicopter one goes from tropical rainforest to desert in only a minute of time. There are black sand, white sand, gold sand, and even green sand beaches. Waterfalls are everywhere along the Hamakua Coast and in the Kohala Mountains. You can fly from the snows of Mauna Kea to the fire of Kilauea. The volcano has been performing daily for over eight years, and while almost everyone would like it to stop, it is always spectacular.

All the photos in this book were done from helicopters. I want to especially thank the pilots who flew me around. Their skill and patience were as amazing as the scenery. Most of the photography was done with Waili Simon of Io Aviation in a Hughes 500. My special gratitude to him for sharing his knowledge of the island. I also went atop the summit of Mauna Kea and along the Kona and Kohala coasts with Kenai Helicopter pilots Raz Rasmussen and Paul Morris in a Bell Ranger. My last flight for this book was with Hilde Lind from Koa Aviation in a Robinson 22. They had just received this two-seater helicopter, which is ideal for photography work.

All of the photography was done with a Pentax 67 medium format camera using a gyroscope. The lenses used were 45mm, 55mm, 75mm, and 135mm.

Douglas Peebles

Photography by Douglas Peebles
Produced by Bennett Hymer
Text by Glen Grant
Corporate Liaison:
    Galyn Wong

Art Direction and Design by
    Fred Bechlen and
    Leo Gonzalez
Design Assistants:
    Stephanie Choy
    Darlene Koning-Tokunaga
    Anna Maniago
Maps: Christine Wilhite /
    Time2Design

Typeset by Typehouse Hawaii
Headlines: Futura Extra Black
Text: Baskerville Roman
Captions: Baskerville Italic

Printed and Bound in Taiwan